COMMISSIONED

GOD'S CALL TO EVERY BELIEVER, NOT JUST THE PASTOR

A Devotional Guide to Living

Your Faith in Any Profession

MICHAEL A. REAHL

DEDICATION

To every believer serving in uniform, in hospitals, and in homes, you are already commissioned. May your life be a living testimony of God's presence in the field where He has placed you.

PREFACE

I never planned to write a book about evangelism. I was simply a young man who had seen enough of the world to know that it could be better, and that the difference was Christ.

My early years were filled with noise, hardship, and influences that pulled me in every direction. When I became a Seventh-day Adventist at the start of the year 2000, everything began to change. I learned discipline, purpose, and a love for Scripture.

I also discovered a truth that would shape my understanding of ministry: you do not have to stand behind a pulpit to serve God. It was near the end of my senior year of high school that I met a stranger who told me this truth that I would never forget: "You do not have to be officially at the pulpit or a pastor to work for the Lord." That single statement stayed with me through the years as I worked as a firefighter, paramedic, police officer, and soldier.

Jesus Himself was not trained in the temple or among the religious elite. He was a carpenter's son who swept floors, cut wood, and served His community long before He preached in the synagogue. Yet when He spoke, people recognized divine authority. His life reminds us that God calls ordinary men and women to do extraordinary things, not through position, but through presence.

In every role I have served, whether carrying a Bible or a badge, I have seen that ministry often happens most powerfully outside the church walls. Evangelism is not limited to preachers or missionaries. It is seen in the medic who treats a patient with compassion, in the officer who prays quietly before entering danger, in the soldier who carries light into dark places, and in the neighbor who listens and serves without expecting anything in return.

The modern church often misunderstands what evangelism truly is. Many believe it only happens through mission trips, church programs, or sermons. Yet true evangelism is the daily reflection of Christ's character in how we live, speak, and treat others. It is both word and witness, truth lived before it is ever spoken.

When Jesus said, "Go therefore and make disciples of all nations" (Matthew 28:19), He was not giving a command to a select group of clergy. He was commissioning every believer. From fishermen to tax collectors, from the educated to the ordinary, His call extends to all who follow Him. That is the message of this book.

I have met many people who underestimate their calling because they do not hold a title. Yet Scripture never limited evangelism to titles; it called for testimonies. The Great Commission is not a task to be assigned but a life to be lived. Your mission field is wherever God has placed your feet, be it in an office, a classroom, a patrol car, or a field; you are already standing in your mission field.

As I studied theology and pursued my Master of Divinity in Biblical Languages, my conviction grew stronger. Every doctrine, every verse, every law of health, and every commandment points to one truth: God's law of love must be lived, not merely learned. When that law is lived, it transforms the believer and everyone around them.

This book is written to make that calling clear. Inside these pages, you will not find abstract ideas, but scriptural foundations, line upon line, precept upon precept, that reveal God's purpose for His people. You will also find practical lessons drawn from everyday experiences and biblical principles applied to real life.

You do not need a theology degree to understand this message. You only need a heart that is willing to listen and a desire to live for Christ.

Before you begin, I invite you to pause and pray. Ask God to open your eyes to see your life through His mission. You have been called, not later, not someday, but now.

This is not a book about preaching. It is a book about living the Gospel. The lessons that follow are drawn from real-life moments in the field, in uniform, and in daily service, where faith had to become action. The goal is simple: to help believers understand that evangelism is not a role for a few but a calling for everyone. When the Gospel becomes the pattern of your character, your entire life turns into a sermon that no pulpit could contain.

Evangelism begins with awareness. The moment you realize that your ordinary life is the stage where heaven and earth meet, everything changes. This book begins there, with that awareness, and walks through what it truly means to live commissioned in a modern world.

May the Spirit of God, who moved fishermen to leave their nets, move you now to see that your world, your home, your workplace, and your community, are your mission field.

Welcome to *Commissioned.*

Note to the Reader

This book is written to encourage every believer, regardless of title or position, to live as a daily witness of God's love and truth. Each chapter is meant to strengthen your faith, deepen your understanding of Scripture, and remind you that evangelism is not confined to pulpits or programs. It is a lifestyle of obedience and compassion, lived wherever God has placed you. The reader may apply the message from this book in his/her devotional time. It may also be helpful in discussing with others in small groups or evangelism training of lay ministers. May these pages inspire you to live commissioned: faithfully, courageously, and with the steady confidence that God's presence works through you.

Author's Note on Sources

Throughout this book, select quotations and ideas are drawn from respected Christian writers such as Martyn Lloyd-Jones and Phil Johnson to reinforce key principles of faith and evangelism. These authors are referenced, not for their theological perspectives, but for their insights on integrity, courage, and biblical authority that align with the spirit of this message revealed in the Word of God. Their inclusion is not a doctrinal endorsement but an acknowledgment of shared biblical convictions that uplift Christ and encourage faithful living. Each source has been prayerfully considered to strengthen the reader's understanding of Scripture and its practical call to witness.[1]

---

1 Select quotations are adapted from Martyn Lloyd-Jones, The Christian Soldier: Standing Firm in the Faith (Baker Books, 2003); and Phil Johnson, Theology Matters (GraceLife, 2007). These are cited for their emphasis on integrity, truth, and biblical conviction.

WRITING AND THEOLOGICAL FRAMEWORK

(How to Read and Apply This Book)

This book is written to inspire believers that ministry is not confined to the pulpit; for every home, workplace, and uniformed duty post is a mission field. It calls men and women of every profession to live as daily witnesses of God's character and truth.

Biblical evangelism is:

- Rooted in truth, confirmed by multiple Scriptures.
- Lived in action, not just spoken.
- Empowered by the Spirit, not human effort.
- Validated by the pioneers, consistent with historic Adventist faith.

Writing Framework

Each chapter follows a four-part devotional structure:

1. **Biblical Foundation** — Presents two or three confirming Scriptures to establish the teaching ("at the witness of two or three a thing is established").
2. **Doctrine** — Explains the doctrine clearly, showing its harmony with the Bible and early Adventist teaching.
3. **Practical Living** — Shows how the truth applies to everyday life: in military, law enforcement, health, and community service.
4. **Reflection** — Ends with a prayerful or reflective thought that challenges readers to live out their faith and share the truth.

Theological Foundations

- The Bible is the complete, sufficient, and final authority for truth, correction, and instruction in righteousness (2 Timothy 3:16–17).
- Evangelism is the heart of Christianity, as it involves proclaiming the gospel and living it out through transformed lives.

Every believer is called to personal evangelism, not just ordained ministers. The gospel's purpose is to reveal God's character, redeem humanity, and restore obedience to God's will.

Evangelism includes compassionate service: health, healing, and helping others in Christ's name.

The Holy Spirit, the Spirit of Truth, empowers all evangelistic work.

Adventist Historical Foundation

This book honors the convictions of early Seventh-day Adventist pioneers who understood evangelism as the shared duty of all believers:

- Ellen G. White: Evangelism is the lifework of every believer; ministers must train members for service.[2]
- James White: Organization exists to advance the gospel; every believer is to be "a living preacher of the truth."
- Joseph Bates: The command "Go ye into all the world" applies to all.
- J. N. Andrews: Every person who has received light must share it.
- Uriah Smith: Ordinary members should distribute truth through personal and printed ministry.
- John N. Loughborough: Every church member is a missionary for Christ.
- John Harvey Kellogg: Health and healing are evangelistic acts fol-

2 Ellen G. White, Evangelism (Review and Herald Publishing Association, 2002), 15.

lowing Christ's example.

Biblical Foundations of Evangelism

The following Scriptures form the anchor points for this book's teachings. Take time to read and reflect on these verses before beginning. Becoming familiar with them will help you understand the purpose and direction of this book. Each one reveals a part of the mission, the power, and the urgency of living a life that is fully commissioned for God.

Commission: Matthew 28:18–20; Mark 16:15; Acts 1:8

Transformation: Romans 12:2; 2 Corinthians 5:17

Every Believer's Role: 1 Peter 2:9; Ephesians 4:12

Personal Outreach: Acts 20:20; Luke 8:39; Matthew 25:35–36

Power Source: Zechariah 4:6; Acts 2:41

Urgency: Revelation 14:6–12; Romans 13:11

Tone and Style

The tone throughout is devotional, pastoral, and reflective, not academic or argumentative. It emphasizes obedience born from love, not legalism.

Every chapter is written in plain, clear language, designed to speak to soldiers, medics, police officers, and everyday believers who serve in their own field. The goal is not theological debate but spiritual transformation, a living call to embody the Great Commission wherever God has placed you.

CHAPTER
ONE

EVANGELISM DEFINED AND LIVED

Biblical Foundation

When Jesus said, "Go therefore and make disciples of all nations" (Matthew 28:19–20), He was not limiting this call to ministers or church officers. He was speaking to every believer who receives the life of God through His Son. The Great Commission is the heartbeat of Heaven flowing through human lives. The Father sent the Son; now, the Son sends His followers with that same spirit of mercy and truth.[3]

The authority of this call does not rest in human wisdom but in the Word of God. Scripture stands as the final measure of truth and the unchanging guide for faith and practice. The Bible is not merely a record of God's works; it is His living voice. As Paul wrote, "All Scripture is breathed out by God and profitable for teaching, for reproof, for correction, and for training in righteousness" (2 Timothy 3:16). Evangelism begins with confidence in the divine authority of the Word. Without it, there is no message to proclaim and no truth to stand on.

Evangelism is not an invention of man but the heartbeat of God Himself.[4] From Genesis to Revelation, the Scriptures reveal a divine pursuit: the Creator calling His creation back to Himself. Jesus declared, "Go therefore and make disciples of all nations, baptizing them in the name of the Father and of the Son and of the Holy Spirit, teaching them to observe all that I have commanded you" (Matthew 28:19–20). This command was not limited to the apostles; it marked the beginning of a movement that continues through every believer who carries the gospel forward.

From the earliest days of the faith, ordinary people carried the message forward. Acts 8:4 tells us, "They that were scattered abroad went every-

---

3 Michael Green, *Evangelism in the Early Church* (Eerdmans, 2004), 18.

4 Alvin Reid, *Introduction to Evangelism* (B&H Publishing Group, 1998), 25–26.

where preaching the word." They had no credentials, no pulpits, only conviction. What gave their words power was not their position, but the Spirit of God, the very presence of the Father and the Son working in and through them.

The gospel itself is the good news of God's grace revealed in Jesus Christ. "For I delivered to you as of first importance what I also received: that Christ died for our sins in accordance with the Scriptures, that he was buried, that he was raised on the third day in accordance with the Scriptures" (1 Corinthians 15:3–4). This message, salvation by grace through faith in Christ alone, defines true evangelism and separates it from every other movement or philosophy.

Before Christ ascended, He promised, "Lo, I am with you always, even unto the end of the world" (Matthew 28:20). That promise was fulfilled when the Father poured out His own Spirit, the life and influence of both Himself and His Son, upon the believers at Pentecost. It was the living presence of God sent through His Son to dwell in His people that descended on the disciples that day (John 14:23; Romans 8:9–11).[5]

Evangelism, therefore, begins with the indwelling presence of God. It is His life reproduced in ours, His character reflected through human hearts.[6] Without that indwelling, words are empty; with it, even the simplest testimony carries Heaven's power.

When Jesus spoke, creation itself obeyed. The wind ceased, the sea grew calm, and spirits fled at His command. His words carried divine life because the Spirit of God was in Him without measure.

Mark 4:39 - "He arose and rebuked the wind, and said to the sea, 'Peace, be still.' And the wind ceased, and there was a great calm."

---

5 Ellen G. White, *The Desire of Ages* (Pacific Press, 1898), 827.

6 Alvin Reid, *Introduction to Evangelism* (B&H Publishing Group, 1998), 22–23.

Matthew 8:26 - "Then He arose and rebuked the winds and the sea; and there was a great calm."

Luke 4:36 - "For with authority and power He commands the unclean spirits, and they come out."

These verses show that Jesus' authority flowed from the divine presence within Him. In the same way, evangelism is powerless without God's indwelling Spirit. Words alone cannot transform, but when His life fills the heart, even the simplest testimony becomes a channel of divine power.

Doctrine – What Evangelism Truly Is

Proclamation and Manifestation: Two Expressions of One Work

Evangelism finds its full meaning in these two divine expressions: *Proclamation* and *Manifestation*. Together, they form the complete witness of a believer who walks in union with the Father through His Son.

Proclamation

To proclaim is to declare the good news that "God was in Christ, reconciling the world unto Himself" (2 Corinthians 5:19). It is the joyful announcement that through the Son, the Father has opened the way for fallen humanity to return to Him. This message is not man's invention but Heaven's invitation, an appeal from the heart of God to the hearts of His children.

When you proclaim, you speak as a messenger of reconciliation. Your words testify that the Father's mercy is greater than sin, that forgiveness has been secured through the sacrifice of His Son, and that eternal life is freely given to all who believe. Proclamation is not argument; it is witness. It is declaring what God has done for you and through you, giving glory to His name.

Manifestation

But proclamation alone is not enough. Words without life are like sound without spirit. Evangelism must also be manifested: embodied in a life transformed by God's own presence. The same God who speaks truth through your mouth must also reveal love through your actions.

This is the work of what Scripture calls "the Spirit of truth," the very life and power of the Father flowing through His Son into all who believe. Jesus promised this when He said, "I will come to you…and My Father will love him, and We will come unto him and make Our abode with him" (John 14:18, 23). The Spirit is that abiding presence, the living connection that makes obedience possible and love visible.

Manifestation is what happens when the truth spoken becomes the truth lived. It is the visible expression of invisible grace. The believer who abides in Christ becomes a branch through which divine life bears fruit: "for without Me," Jesus said, "you can do nothing" (John 15:5). Every act of kindness, patience, and purity becomes evidence that the Father's Spirit dwells within.

In this way, evangelism is not something we perform but something we become. It is the Father working through the Son, and the Son working through us. As Paul wrote, "It is God who works in you, both to will and to do of His good pleasure" (Philippians 2:13). When God's will becomes our desire, and His love becomes our motive, the Gospel is proclaimed with power and manifested with purity.

The world has heard many sermons, but it longs to see living ones. Every believer whose life reflects the character of Christ preaches a message that Heaven celebrates. Jesus said, "There is joy before the angels of God over one sinner who repents" (Luke 15:10). Each time a soul turns toward God, all of Heaven rejoices. The angels are not distant observers, for Scripture says, "Are they not all ministering spirits sent out to serve for the sake of those who are to inherit salvation?" (Hebrews 1:14). They gladly join in the work of redemption, serving beside those who live and witness for Christ. When our lives reveal His love, we become part of this divine partnership, bringing joy to Heaven and glory to the God who saves.

Practical Living – Evangelism in Everyday Life

Your mission field begins right where you stand. You may never travel across oceans, but every place you walk is ground that God can claim through you. The person beside you at work, the neighbor across the street, the friend who shares a burden, these are all within the reach of your influence.

Paul wrote, "Whatever you do, work heartily, as for the Lord and not for men" (Colossians 3:23). Every honest task becomes sacred when done with the consciousness that the Father sees you and empowers you through His Spirit. The nurse who comforts, the officer who protects, the mechanic who serves with integrity are all ministers of righteousness when moved by divine love.

Christ's presence in the believer transforms the ordinary into the holy. When the Spirit of God guides your words, even casual conversation can turn hearts toward Heaven. When His peace rules your reactions, others catch a glimpse of the kingdom within. The Father's life, flowing through His Son into you, becomes a living testimony far stronger than any argument.

Evangelism does not demand eloquence; it requires awareness. Ask each morning, "Father, dwell in me through Your Spirit; live Your life through my hands today." With that prayer, you will find divine appointments everywhere: a hurting soul needing comfort, a moment of tension calling for calm, a question that opens the door to truth.

Jesus' early years teach this lesson. Before He ever preached, He labored faithfully in the carpenter's shop. There, He revealed the dignity of labor and the holiness of daily duty. So too the believer, no matter if you're wearing a uniform or carrying a toolbox, shows the beauty of Heaven in the discipline of earth.

Reflection – Living the Message

Evangelism is not a program to complete but a divine partnership with God Himself. Jesus said, *"As the Father has sent me, even so I am sending you"* (John 20:21). Just as the Father sent His Son into the world to reveal His character and redeem humanity, He now sends His children to continue that same mission. Through the same Spirit that filled Christ, the Father extends His presence once more to the world, this time through His people. Scripture declares, *"All this is from God, who through Christ reconciled us to himself and gave us the ministry of reconciliation"* (2 Corinthians 5:18). Evangelism, therefore, is the ongoing heartbeat of Heaven, where redeemed lives become living testimonies of God's redeeming love.

Ask yourself:

How can God's life shine through mine today?

Jesus said, "You are the light of the world" (Matthew 5:14). Light does not strive; it simply reveals. So, let the Father's light, reflected through His Son, radiate from your character. Speak truth with gentleness, serve with humility, forgive freely, and walk uprightly. Such a life cannot be hidden.

You have been called to more than belief; you have been called to representation. The Father desires to make His appeal through you. This is evangelism: God in you, the hope of glory.

Evangelism flows from relationship, not obligation. The more we know the Savior, the more we reflect His heart to the world. The call to share is not a duty to perform but a joy to live out. In every place, whether in uniform, in a classroom, or in a quiet home, God seeks willing hearts through whom He can speak life.

You are not waiting to be sent; you already are.

Live commissioned, today and every day, until the whole earth is filled with the knowledge of the Lord.

CHAPTER
TWO

THE MISSION FIELD AROUND YOU

Biblical Foundation

When Jesus spoke of the harvest, He wasn't referring only to faraway lands. He was speaking of the souls all around us, the people in our homes, workplaces, and communities who long for hope and truth. "Lift up your eyes, and look on the fields; for they are white already to harvest" (John 4:35).

From Genesis to Revelation, the concept of harvest carries deep spiritual significance. In the Old Testament, harvest symbolized God's provision and faithfulness (Deuteronomy 8:7–10; Psalm 65:9–13). Yet, it also carried responsibility: gathering what God had provided, sharing with the poor, and offering the firstfruits back to Him.

When Jesus used the image of harvest, He elevated it from physical work to spiritual mission.[7] After speaking with the Samaritan woman, He told His disciples, "Behold, I say to you, lift up your eyes and look at the fields, for they are already white for harvest" (John 4:35). The disciples saw an outsider; Jesus saw potential. They saw difference; He saw redemption.

The same call comes to every believer. The harvest is not far from us; it surrounds us daily. When Jesus said, "The harvest truly is plentiful, but the laborers are few" (Matthew 9:37), it was not a complaint, but a commissioning. He invited His followers to see the world through Heaven's eyes, to notice those whom others overlook.

This awareness begins with purity of heart. The early church's effectiveness was born from holiness and integrity. Before God sent them outward, He purified them inwardly. As Acts 5 shows, sin threatened to destroy the power of their witness until the Spirit corrected it. Evange-

---

7 Robert E. Webber, *The Younger Evangelicals* (Baker Books, 2002), 94–95.

lism that flows from an impure life loses credibility. The world must first see the transforming power of Christ within us before it can believe the message we proclaim.

Every conversation, every encounter, every task is part of that harvest field. The crying coworker, the weary cashier, the lonely neighbor, each one is an opportunity to gather souls for the kingdom.[8]

Doctrine – The Everyday Mission Field

Evangelism is not defined by geography but by opportunity. The early church spread because ordinary believers shared the gospel wherever they went.[9] "They that were scattered abroad went everywhere preaching the word" (Acts 8:4). The same Spirit that empowered them now empowers us.

Your mission field is wherever the Father has placed you. Some are called to distant lands, while others are called to their own neighborhoods. Paul wrote, *"Let each person lead the life that the Lord has assigned to him, and to which God has called him"* (1 Corinthians 7:17). God strategically places us in barracks, classrooms, hospitals, patrol cars, and offices to be His witnesses in places others cannot reach.

I remember in the early 2000s, a small book by Bruce Wilkinson titled *The Prayer of Jabez* caught my attention. Many understood it as a message of prosperity, but the heart of Jabez's prayer was really about spiritual influence and faithful outreach. He prayed, *"Oh that you would bless me and enlarge my border, and that your hand might be with me"* (1 Chronicles 4:10). Jabez desired his life to have a greater impact for God's purposes. In the same way, when we ask God to enlarge our borders, we are asking Him to

---

8 *Michael Green, Evangelism in the Early Church* (Grand Rapids, MI: Eerdmans, 2003), 47.

9 Michael Green, *Evangelism in the Early Church* (Wm. B. Eerdmans, 2004), 35–36.

expand our mission field and open doors for His love and truth to reach others through us.

But the hand of God upon us is not just for blessing; it is for boldness. Acts 4:29–31 shows believers praying, "Grant to Your servants to continue to speak Your word with all boldness." This boldness was not human courage but the result of the Holy Spirit's power. Evangelism does not thrive on self-confidence; it thrives on Spirit-dependence. Our mission fields are conquered not by persuasive personalities, but by divine power flowing through surrendered hearts.

The gospel travels best through relationships.[10] Jesus ministered not from a distance but within the daily lives of people, dining with sinners, teaching fishermen, healing the sick, speaking with outcasts. Evangelism begins the same way for us, not in a pulpit, but in the flow of life.

In every generation, the gospel faces resistance, and that resistance refines its messengers. The apostles were persecuted, yet their suffering became a platform for greater witness (Acts 5:41–42). When opposition arises, it is not proof that God has left us, but that His light is confronting darkness. Persecution does not stop evangelism; it purifies it.

To see your mission field, pray as Jesus did: "Open their eyes." When your eyes open to the needs around you, you will see what Heaven sees: souls ready for harvest.

Practical Living – Where You Stand Is Holy Ground

Your uniform, your work badge, and your title are not barriers to ministry; they are extensions of it. The believer who works with integrity and compassion testifies more powerfully than any sermon.[11]

10 Jan Paulsen, *When the Spirit Descends* (Pacific Press, 1998), 56.

11 *Ellen G. White, The Ministry of Healing* (Mountain View, CA: Pacific

The classroom teacher, the paramedic, the soldier, and the nurse all share the same opportunity: to represent Christ through their character. When you perform your duties faithfully, speak truthfully, and treat others with kindness, you plant gospel seeds.

Evangelism in daily life requires persistence. The early believers "did not cease teaching and preaching Jesus as the Christ" (Acts 5:42). Even in the face of threats and suffering, they continued. Persistence proves love; it shows that our message is not just a seasonal enthusiasm, but a lifelong devotion. When we keep witnessing through fatigue, misunderstanding, or indifference, God turns our endurance into eternal fruit.

A smile, a word of encouragement, or a moment of listening are small gestures that can open eternal doors. Many may never step into a church, but they will meet Christ in you.

When God called Moses from the burning bush, He said, "Take off your sandals, for the place where you stand is holy ground" (Exodus 3:5). Holiness was not in the soil but in the presence of God. Wherever you stand in obedience and service, that place becomes holy.

In military life, police work, or medicine, we often meet people in crisis. Each crisis is a crossroads where light and darkness meet. How you respond with compassion, calm, and prayer, can turn a moment of pain into a divine encounter.

When you see your workplace as your mission field, evangelism stops being an event and becomes a lifestyle.

Reflection – Lift Up Your Eyes

Jesus never asked His disciples to go where He hadn't already gone. He calls us to see as He sees, with compassion that transcends boundaries.

Press, 1905), 470.

True evangelism holds fast to two unshakable truths: Scripture alone defines our message, and faith alone brings salvation. Our task is not to invent new ideas but to proclaim the Word that cannot be broken (John 10:35). When we remain faithful to Scripture and trust in its power, we labor with Heaven's authority. That is why the apostles said, "We cannot but speak of what we have seen and heard" (Acts 4:20). Their conviction came from revelation, not from opinion.

Take a moment each day to pray: "Lord, open my eyes to the harvest around me." You will begin to notice the quiet burdens people carry. You will see how your actions, words, and prayers fit into God's larger plan of redemption.

The harvest is not waiting; it is already happening. You are not a spectator; you are a laborer. Every conversation can plant a seed, every kind act can water it, and every prayer can bring it to life.

Lift up your eyes. The field before you is white for harvest.

Live commissioned, and gather for the Kingdom.

CHAPTER

THREE

FAITH IN UNIFORM: LIVING FOR CHRIST IN YOUR PROFESSION

Biblical Foundation

The Bible never separates faith from daily life. From Joseph in Egypt to Daniel in Babylon, God's people have always been called to live faithfully in environments that test integrity and courage. As Colossians 3:23 reminds us, "Whatever you do, work heartily, as for the Lord and not for men."

Faith in Uniform: Whether that uniform belongs to a soldier, an officer, a nurse, or a laborer, it means representing Christ under pressure. It means carrying truth into spaces where compromise and darkness try to rule.

Before a believer can represent Christ outwardly, their heart must first be right before God. True ministry begins with purity. A life in uniform, without a cleansed heart, becomes hypocrisy. Scripture reminds us in 2 Timothy 2:19, "Let everyone who names the name of the Lord depart from iniquity." The credibility of your witness depends on the integrity of your walk. The world respects consistency more than words; it must see holiness behind the badge, behind the rank, behind the title.

When I was in high school, I worked at Walt Disney World in Orlando. We were called cast members, and during interviews, each person was asked if they could act out their role. Whether you were a custodian, a shopkeeper, or an ice cream vendor, the question was always the same: "Can you perform this role?" That question has stayed with me because, in many ways, it reflects our calling as believers. God places us in different roles and expects us to live them with excellence and integrity, not for applause, but for His glory. Every uniform, every position, becomes a platform for witness. Wherever God assigns us, we are called to live out our faith so that others see His character through our actions.

Christ Himself modeled this. Before preaching on hillsides or calming storms, He spent thirty years in ordinary labor under divine discipline. His hidden years in the carpenter's shop were years of preparation, where obedience in the small things laid the foundation for faithfulness in the greater. Evangelism grows from the same soil of daily obedience that turns work into worship.

Jesus Himself grew up as a laborer. Before teaching in synagogues or performing miracles, He worked with His hands in a carpenter's shop. His life teaches us that ministry begins in faithfulness, not fame. Every act of service done with love and integrity is sacred.

This truth separates the shallow from the steadfast. Many want to serve God publicly, but few are willing to serve Him privately. The believer in uniform learns that quiet excellence speaks louder than self-promotion. As Matthew 5:16 tells us, "Let your light shine before others, so that they may see your good works and give glory to your Father who is in heaven." In that unseen faithfulness, God's power rests.

The uniformed believer stands as both servant and witness. Like the centurion in Matthew 8, who recognized authority and humility, a person in service reflects the order and discipline of Heaven. When you wear your uniform with humility and purpose, you carry the presence of Christ into the world.[12]

Doctrine – Vocation as Calling

God never separates the sacred from the secular. He sanctifies every honest calling. Paul reminds us that "we are ambassadors for Christ, as though God were making His appeal through us" (2 Corinthians 5:20).

Your profession is not separate from your faith; it is the very platform God has given you to live it. To the believer, every uniform becomes a form of ministry vestment. Every title, from medic to mechanic, becomes an assignment from Heaven.

---

12 *Alan Kreider, The Patient Ferment of the Early Church* (Grand Rapids, MI: Baker Academic, 2016), 89.

Evangelism in vocation demands conviction. Truth cannot be compromised to gain approval. Lloyd-Jones said that fidelity to the gospel means declaring both what we believe and what we reject.[13] A believer who bends truth to fit culture loses moral authority.[14] Scripture commands, "Stand therefore, having fastened on the belt of truth" (Ephesians 6:14). In every profession, truth must stay fastened, or the witness unravels.

When Christ lives within you, your duty becomes a sermon. Compassion, fairness, and courage preach louder than words. Faithful service becomes an altar where God's character is revealed.

Faith in uniform requires balance, strength with gentleness, authority with humility.[15] The believer learns to serve under authority and to lead by example, reflecting the heart of the One who came "not to be served but to serve" (Matthew 20:28).

God's Spirit enables you to live above reproach in systems often marked by temptation, corruption, or weariness. In your work ethic, others see stability; in your reactions, they see peace; in your compassion, they see Christ.

When your faith meets opposition in the workplace, remember the apostles' example: "They left the presence of the council, rejoicing that they were counted worthy to suffer dishonor for the name" (Acts 5:41). Persecution is not a setback but a seal of authenticity. God uses resistance to refine the messenger and magnify the message. When others see steadfastness under pressure, they recognize a strength not of this world.

---

13 Martyn Lloyd-Jones, *The Christian Soldier: Standing Firm in the Faith* (Grand Rapids, MI: Baker Books, 2003), 47.

14 D. Martyn Lloyd-Jones, *What Is an Evangelical?* (Edinburgh: Banner of Truth Trust, 1992), 54–55.

15 Martyn Lloyd-Jones, *Preaching and Preachers* (Zondervan, 1971), 71.

Practical Living – Witnessing Through Example

A soldier on patrol, a police officer responding to a call, a nurse comforting a patient, each of these moments is an opportunity to show the heart of God. You may never preach a sermon, but your actions declare your faith every day.

Ask yourself: If my coworkers never hear me speak of Christ, will they still see Him in me?

Faith in uniform does not mean quoting Scripture at every turn. It means *living Scripture.* It is showing integrity when no one is watching, speaking truth even when it costs, and treating every person with the dignity of one created in God's image.

Consistency turns testimony into trust. The world measures truth by repetition; when your character remains steady under fatigue, frustration, and failure, people begin to believe your faith is real. As Galatians 6:9 reminds us, "Let us not grow weary of doing good, for in due season we will reap, if we do not give up." Persistence in righteousness is the everyday miracle of evangelism.

In moments of conflict or stress, pause and pray: "Lord, let Your Spirit rule my response." When the world expects anger, answer with calm. When it expects judgment, respond with mercy. These quiet victories display divine strength.

Every believer in uniform becomes a light in places others cannot go. When a patient is dying, when a victim is afraid, when a recruit feels lost, your faith may be the only sermon they ever encounter.

Faith in uniform is more than endurance; it is representation. It says to the world, "God's presence dwells here, even in this uniform, even in this environment."

Reflection – Living the Gospel in the Field

The world measures success by rank and recognition. God measures it by faithfulness.

True success in evangelism is measured not by visible results but by obedience to truth. Scripture never commands us to convert; it commands us to proclaim. As Luke 17:10 says, "We are unworthy servants; we have only done what was our duty." Heaven records faithfulness, while earth sees routine.

You may not always see the fruit of your labor, but Heaven does. Every quiet prayer, every honest report, and every act of mercy are recorded as eternal testimonies.

Pray each day: "Father, help me to wear this uniform as Your servant. Let my strength reflect Your justice and my compassion reveal Your love."

When your heart aligns with Heaven, the field you serve becomes sacred ground. You are not simply performing duty; you are carrying divine presence into human struggle.

Faith in uniform is not just about standing tall; it is about kneeling low before God. That humility becomes your greatest strength, and your service becomes worship.

You are a living witness, commissioned in uniform, faithful in service, and shining as a light in the midst of the field.

CHAPTER
FOUR

EVANGELISM BY EXAMPLE: LET YOUR LIFE SPEAK

Biblical Foundation

Jesus said, *"You are the light of the world. A city set on a hill cannot be hidden."* (Matthew 5:14). Light does not argue; it simply shines. That is the heart of evangelism by example, living in such a way that others see the difference Christ has made in you before you ever explain it.

Light cannot be borrowed; it must be kindled by truth. The believer's radiance depends on the purity of heart. Jesus said, "Blessed are the pure in heart, for they shall see God" (Matthew 5:8). The more clearly we see Him, the more brightly we reflect Him. Compromise dims that witness; holiness sharpens it. Evangelism by example begins when the inner life is surrendered to God's refining presence.

This calling to shine did not begin in the New Testament. The prophets spoke of it long before: *"Arise, shine, for your light has come, and the glory of the Lord has risen upon you… and nations shall come to your light"* (Isaiah 60:1–3). God's people were always meant to reflect His glory to the world. Proverbs says, *"The path of the righteous is like the light of dawn, which shines brighter and brighter until full day."* (Proverbs 4:18). The more a person walks with God, the clearer His light becomes through them.

Peter echoed this truth when he urged believers, *"Keep your conduct honorable, so that when they speak against you, they may see your good deeds and glorify God."* (1 Peter 2:12). The first century church grew because people witnessed transformed lives, neighbors sharing food, caring for the sick, and treating one another with unusual kindness. Their actions became their message, just as God intended from the beginning.

This purity and consistency of life gave the early believers power in their proclamation. They did not persuade through argument but through transformation. Their witness could not be dismissed because it was visible. "By this all people will know that you are my disciples, if you have love for one another" (John 13:35). Evangelism by example is love made visible.

Doctrine: Character as a Message

Evangelism was never designed to rely on eloquence alone; it depends on evidence, the visible change in a believer's life.

Paul told the Corinthians, *"You yourselves are our letter, written not with ink but with the Spirit of the living God."* (2 Corinthians 3:3).

Our lives are living letters. The messenger must match the message.

Doctrine without character is noise, but character without doctrine is confusion. The power of evangelism rests on both truth and transformation. Paul reminded Timothy, "Keep a close watch on yourself and on the teaching. Persist in this, for by so doing you will save both yourself and your hearers" (1 Timothy 4:16). The Spirit works through lives that are both pure and biblically grounded.

Words lose power when conduct contradicts them, but when truth and character align, the Spirit magnifies the witness far beyond human effort.

To live by example means being the same person in private and in public; honest, patient, forgiving, and pure in motive. Authenticity is the loudest sermon.

The credibility of our faith is not tested by applause but by adversity. The apostles' lives were open letters written in suffering. "We are afflicted in every way, but not crushed; perplexed, but not driven to despair" (2 Corinthians 4:8). Their endurance proved their message. Evangelism by example shines brightest in hardship because it demonstrates that faith holds when everything else fails.

Practical Living: Everyday Sermons

Every believer preaches, whether intentionally or not. Coworkers notice your reactions under pressure. Family members learn the Gospel through your patience and kindness. Strangers recognize Christ when they feel your compassion.

- **At work:** Integrity is evangelism. Doing your duty with honesty when shortcuts tempt you speaks volumes.

- **In community:** Kindness is evangelism. A gentle response, a shared meal, or a quiet prayer reveals God's love more clearly than debate.

- **In hardship:** Faithfulness is evangelism. Continuing to trust God when life hurts becomes a testimony stronger than words.

Consistency is your pulpit. "Let your speech always be gracious, seasoned with salt, so that you may know how you ought to answer each person" (Colossians 4:6). Even silence can speak when it reflects peace instead of pride. When your life and language align, you preach a sermon Heaven honors.

You do not need a pulpit to preach; only consistency. The light of Christ within you does not need to be announced; it needs to be seen.

Reflection: The Silent Sermon

Ask yourself: *If someone only watched my life, would they still learn who Christ is?*

Your habits, words, and attitude are shaping someone's perception of God.

The Christian life is a continual proclamation. We do not choose whether to represent Christ; we only choose how well we do it. Paul wrote, "We are the aroma of Christ to God among those who are being saved and among those who are perishing" (2 Corinthians 2:15). Some will be drawn to the fragrance; others will reject it, but all will notice it.

Be faithful when unseen, gentle when provoked, and steadfast when weary. Your calm endurance may lead another soul to hope.

Let your life be the pulpit where Christ is seen.

Live in such a way that others glorify God simply because they crossed paths with you.

Evangelism by example is not passive; it is persistent holiness. Keep shining when it costs you comfort. Keep forgiving when pride whispers otherwise. Light is never wasted; every act of faithfulness becomes a reflection of God's mercy to someone watching.

When character reflects Christ, our words can carry His Spirit. The next step in evangelism is learning to speak truth with both conviction and compassion.

FIVE

SPEAKING THE TRUTH IN LOVE: GRACE AND CONVICTION IN WITNESS

Biblical Foundation

Paul urged the church in Ephesus to *"speak the truth in love, growing up in every way into Him who is the Head, Christ"* (Ephesians 4:15).

Truth without love becomes harsh. Love without truth becomes hollow. Christ calls His followers to embody both.

Truth is never optional for the believer because it is the reflection of God's own nature. Jesus prayed, "Sanctify them in the truth; your word is truth" (John 17:17). To speak truth in love means allowing Scripture, not emotion or opinion, to govern every word. Love gives truth its tone; truth gives love its strength.

Jesus modeled this perfect balance. He confronted sin but never crushed the sinner. When He spoke with the woman at the well (John 4), His honesty revealed her brokenness, yet His compassion offered healing. The result was transformation; she became a witness to her whole town.

The way we speak often determines whether people will listen to what we say. Evangelism is not only about proclaiming the right message, but also about doing so in the right spirit.

The early church understood this. They spoke boldly, yet humbly, depending on the Spirit to soften hearts. "They were all filled with the Holy Spirit and continued to speak the word of God with boldness" (Acts 4:31). Power and tenderness met together in their witness, proving that love and conviction are not opposites but partners in truth.

Doctrine: Grace and Truth in Harmony

Scripture says that Jesus was *"full of grace and truth"* (John 1:14).

These two divine attributes must never be separated in the life of a believer.

- **Truth** reveals the holiness of God and the standard of righteousness.
- **Grace** reveals the mercy of God and His desire to save.

When we speak truth without love, we can drive people away from the Savior who loves them.

When we offer love without truth, we can leave them comfortable in the sin that destroys them. Evangelism means holding both, confronting error while extending hope.

Grace without truth becomes sentimentalism; truth without grace becomes cruelty. The Spirit of God guards us from both extremes by producing gentleness and courage together. Paul told Timothy, "The Lord's servant must not be quarrelsome but kind to everyone, able to teach, patiently enduring evil, correcting his opponents with gentleness" (2 Timothy 2:24–25). Such correction invites repentance instead of resentment.

The Holy Spirit gives believers discernment to balance conviction with compassion.

A Spirit-led witness does not argue for victory but speaks for redemption. The goal is never to prove someone wrong but to help them find freedom in Christ.

True authority in witness comes from submission, not superiority. The messenger who has knelt before the truth speaks with Heaven's weight. That humility is what makes truth believable.

Practical Living: Conversations that Heal

Evangelism is rarely a speech; it's a conversation guided by love. When you listen before speaking, you earn the right to be heard. When you show understanding instead of judgment, hearts begin to open.

In daily life, speaking truth in love looks like this:

- In correction: Offer truth gently, remembering that you too are growing.
- In testimony: Share Scripture to bring peace, not pressure.
- In dialogue: Talk about faith humbly, not to win but to witness.
- In tone: Let kindness steady your words, even when truth must challenge.

You can share Christ in a patrol car, a classroom, or a quiet conversation over a meal.

A story of your own transformation, or a simple "I'll pray for you," may open more hearts than a sermon.

When your heart is anchored in love, truth will flow naturally because it reflects who you are becoming in Christ.

Sometimes love will cost you. The apostles spoke boldly even when threatened: "We cannot but speak of what we have seen and heard" (Acts 4:20). Their words were not reckless but righteous. Courage is love refusing to stay silent.

Reflection: The Voice of a Witness

Before you speak, ask yourself:

"Will these words bring someone closer to Jesus, or push them further away?"

Every word we speak carries weight. Use yours to build, not to break.

Remember, God did not call us to win arguments; He called us to win souls. Speak with courage, but never without kindness.

Correct with clarity, but always with compassion.

Let every word be seasoned with grace, so that when people hear you, they also feel the presence of Christ.

That is the voice of a true witness, truth spoken in love.

And when truth provokes rejection, do not be discouraged. "If the world hates you, know that it has hated me before it hated you" (John 15:18). Persecution tests whether our love is genuine. Responding with grace under pressure proves that the Spirit, not pride, guides our hearts.

Love and truth prepare the heart for obedience, but obedience often requires courage. Evangelism will test both your faith and your resolve. When love guides our words, our story becomes a doorway to grace.

So keep speaking. Do not retreat into silence or react in anger. Speak the truth in love, again and again, until grace has done its work. Persistence in gentle truth-telling is one of the Spirit's greatest tools for salvation.

CHAPTER

SIX

THE POWER OF PERSONAL TESTIMONY

Biblical Foundation

In every age, God has chosen ordinary people to reveal His extraordinary grace. From the healed man in Mark 5, who was told, "Go home to your friends and tell them how much the Lord has done for you" (Mark 5:19), to Paul standing before kings sharing how Christ changed his life, the pattern is clear: testimony is one of Heaven's most powerful tools.

Scripture is filled with personal accounts of divine intervention: Abraham's obedience, Moses' calling, Ruth's loyalty, Daniel's courage, Mary's faith, and Peter's restoration. These stories teach us that God does not merely speak *to* us; He works *through* us.

Revelation 12:11 declares, "They overcame him by the blood of the Lamb and by the word of their testimony." Victory in the Christian life is not found only in knowing truth but in sharing what that truth has done for us.

A personal testimony is not about perfection; it is about transformation. It is the living evidence that the Spirit of God is real, powerful, and present in human experience.

But testimony loses power when the life behind it contradicts the message. Jesus said, "Let your light shine before others, so that they may see your good works and give glory to your Father who is in heaven" (Matthew 5:16). Purity and testimony are inseparable; a life cleansed by grace becomes the clearest voice for truth. The most convincing witness is not the loudest but the holiest.

Doctrine – The Witness of Experience

The Bible teaches that truth is established "at the witness of two or three" (Deuteronomy 19:15). Testimony is that second witness: the confirmation that God's Word is alive and effective. When you share what

Christ has done in your life, you are not merely recounting memories; you are verifying His promises.

Your story may not be dramatic, but it is divinely appointed. God uses the simple and sincere to touch hearts that the polished words of theology may never reach. A changed life is a sermon that cannot be silenced.

The apostles' preaching always began with testimony; what they had "seen and heard" (Acts 4:20). Their words carried divine power because they were eyewitnesses of grace and vessels of the Spirit. True testimony always points away from self and back to the cross.

Testimony has two parts: **proclamation** and **confirmation**. Proclamation declares what God has said; confirmation demonstrates what He has done. When both exist together, faith becomes visible.

Personal witness is not about defending doctrine but displaying deliverance. It shows

how the gospel moves from theory to transformation. Even under persecution, believers testified boldly because they had experienced the truth firsthand. "We also believe, and so we also speak" (2 Corinthians 4:13).

The enemy of souls works to silence the believer's story. He knows that a shared testimony becomes a spark that lights another life. Yet, as long as we remember who redeemed us, our words carry eternal weight.[16]

Ellen White once wrote that "the strongest argument in favor of the gospel is a loving and lovable Christian."[17] That is testimony: the gospel made visible through the life of the redeemed.

Satan fears a consistent Christian more than a persuasive preacher. A

---

16 *Ellen G. White, The Ministry of Healing* (Mountain View, CA: Pacific Press, 1905), 470.

17 Ibid, 470.

single believer walking in purity can undo years of deception. Your faithfulness, tested and proven, becomes the evidence Hell cannot refute.

Practical Living – Sharing Christ in Your Own Words

Every believer can share the gospel through personal experience. You don't need credentials; you only need authenticity. Speak from the heart. Tell what Christ has done for you.

When someone asks how you keep peace under pressure, that is an open door to testify. When a coworker expresses hopelessness, that is your moment to share hope.

A soldier can testify through courage, a nurse through compassion, an officer through integrity, a teacher through patience. Each life becomes a living message.

There are three simple ways to build your testimony:

1. **Remember what God has done.** Keep a record of answered prayers and changed moments.
2. **Relate it to others naturally.** Speak of faith as part of your everyday life, not as a sermon.
3. **Reflect Christ continually.** Let your behavior confirm your words.

When your life and speech align, people recognize the truth without you having to force it.

Sometimes your testimony will meet resistance. Jesus said, "You will be hated by all for my name's sake. But the one who endures to the end will be saved" (Matthew 10:22). Do not let fear silence what faith has written. Every trial becomes part of the power of your story.

The Samaritan woman at the well had no formal training, but her words brought a town to Jesus: "Come, see a man who told me everything I ever did!" (John 4:29). Her testimony sparked revival.

So it is with you. Your honesty about how God met you in weakness, healed you in pain, or guided you through duty may open hearts more deeply than a thousand sermons.

The Spirit can use even your scars as Scripture; living reminders that grace still works. Do not wait until you feel ready; speak while your heart is tender. God perfects the message through your obedience.

Reflection – Your Story, His Glory

Never underestimate the power of your story. The enemy wants you to stay silent out of fear or shame, but God calls you to speak. Every testimony, no matter how small, magnifies the grace of God and silences the accuser.

When you tell others how Christ changed your life, you're not drawing attention to yourself but to the One who saves.

Pray: "Father, give me courage to speak of Your goodness. Let my story be a bridge for others to know You."

Each word you share becomes part of a greater narrative: the story of redemption still being written through God's people.

Your life is a letter of Christ, written not with ink but by the Spirit of the living God (2 Corinthians 3:3). Let it be read. Let it be seen. Let it glorify Him.

You have a story Heaven cherishes, and the world needs to hear it. Shared light attracts resistance; the next step is learning to stand when witness is costly.

So stand firm. "Do not be ashamed of the testimony about our Lord"

(2 Timothy 1:8). The same Spirit who gave you a story will give you the strength to tell it. When purity guards your heart and the Spirit fills your words, your story becomes not just memory, but ministry.

CHAPTER

SEVEN

THE COST AND COURAGE OF EVANGELISM: STANDING FOR TRUTH IN A CHANGING WORLD

Biblical Foundation

Jesus never promised that following Him would be easy. He said plainly, *"If anyone would come after Me, let him deny himself and take up his cross daily and follow Me"* (Luke 9:23).

True evangelism, living and speaking for Christ, has always come at a cost. It may cost comfort, reputation, or even relationships. But the reward of obedience always outweighs the pain of resistance.

From the earliest disciples to the prophets of old, courage has marked those who answered God's call. Peter and John declared before the council, *"We cannot but speak of what we have seen and heard"* (Acts 4:20).

Paul faced prison, storms, and persecution, yet said, *"Woe to me if I do not preach the Gospel"* (1 Corinthians 9:16).

Courage in evangelism is not human bravery; it is divine strength.[18] It flows from knowing that even when the world opposes truth, Heaven stands with you.

Jesus said, "Blessed are those who are persecuted for righteousness' sake, for theirs is the kingdom of heaven" (Matthew 5:10). The mark of true discipleship is endurance when truth is unpopular. The early believers rejoiced "that they were counted worthy to suffer dishonor for the name." (Acts 5:41). Their courage was not pride but praise, born from knowing that no cost compares to Christ.

Doctrine: Suffering and Strength in the Spirit

The life of a believer is a battlefield between faith and fear. Yet Scripture reminds us, *"God gave us a spirit not of fear, but of power and love and self-control"* (2 Timothy 1:7).

---

18 Martyn Lloyd-Jones, Joy Unspeakable: Power & Renewal in the Holy Spirit (Crossway, 1984), 112.

The Holy Spirit empowers believers to stand when others retreat, to love when others hate, and to speak when silence would be safer.

Every great movement of God required men and women who valued obedience over approval.

Courage, in God's kingdom, is not the absence of fear, it is faith that obeys in spite of fear.

Jeremiah confessed, *"If I say, 'I will not mention Him,' there is in my heart as it were a burning fire shut up in my bones"* (Jeremiah 20:9).

That same fire burns in every believer who cannot remain silent about what Christ has done.

The cost of discipleship refines character. Those who endure learn to depend not on applause but on God's approval. The strength to stand begins with conviction that truth is not ours to edit or soften. Scripture, not culture, defines what we proclaim. Paul charged Timothy, "Preach the word; be ready in season and out of season; reprove, rebuke, and exhort, with complete patience and teaching" (2 Timothy 4:2) . Evangelism loses its power when believers lose their confidence in the Word.

Lloyd-Jones once said that the first sign of a dying church is when it ceases to be clear about what it stands against.[19] Love without conviction becomes compromise, but truth with love becomes courage. To suffer for righteousness is not tragedy; it is testimony that your faith is genuine.[20]

---

19 Martyn Lloyd-Jones, *Preaching and Preachers* (Grand Rapids: Zondervan, 1971), 112.

20 Lloyd-Jones, *What Is an Evangelical?*, 54–55.

Practical Living: Standing Firm in a Hostile World

Modern evangelism faces new forms of opposition, mockery, indifference, or the fear of being misunderstood. But these challenges are not new. Every generation of believers has had to choose between comfort and conviction.

Here's what courage looks like in everyday life:

- At work: Choosing integrity when compromise would be easier.
- In conversation: Mentioning your faith even when others might dismiss it.
- In adversity: Remaining kind when criticized for your beliefs.
- In service: Continuing to love and serve those who misunderstand or mistreat you.

Courage does not always shout from a platform; sometimes it endures quietly with steadfast faith. Both forms honor God when done in love.

Every act of faithfulness is a sermon of courage. When you live boldly for Christ, others will see that your strength comes from beyond yourself.

You are not alone in the battle. The same Spirit who filled Stephen as he faced his accusers fills every believer today. "But he, full of the Holy Spirit, gazed into heaven and saw the glory of God" (Acts 7:55). Courage flows from communion, with eyes fixed not on fear, but on the faithful One who never fails.

Remember that persecution is temporary, but witness is eternal. The scars you bear for truth become eternal trophies of grace. "For this light momentary affliction is preparing for us an eternal weight of glory beyond all comparison" (2 Corinthians 4:17).

Reflection: Fearless Because of Faith

Courage does not mean you never feel afraid, it means you trust God more than your fear.

David wrote, *"The Lord is my light and my salvation; whom shall I fear?"* (Psalm 27:1)

The same God who strengthened David strengthens you today.

When fear rises, remember who sent you. You do not speak by your own authority; you carry the message of the King.

Ask yourself: *What am I willing to lose for Christ's sake?* The honest answer reveals the depth of your faith.

The cost of evangelism refines us, but it also rewards us, with deeper peace, stronger faith, and eternal joy.

When you stand for truth, you never stand alone. The One who commissioned you walks beside you.

Be brave, not because the world is kind, but because God is faithful.

Keep speaking. Keep shining. Keep standing.

Your courage is your testimony.

And remember the promise of Christ: "Everyone who acknowledges me before men, I also will acknowledge before my Father who is in heaven." (Matthew 10:32) One day, every act of courage will echo before the throne. What the world mocked, Heaven will honor. What seemed lost will be crowned with glory.

Biblical Foundation

Before Jesus left His disciples, He gave them a promise that would define the rest of Christian history: "I will ask the Father, and He will give you another Comforter, that He may abide with you forever, the Spirit of truth" (John 14:16–17).

Many have not truly understood this promise. The Spirit of truth, a profound blessing promised to each disciple of Christ, is the very presence of the Father and the Son working within the believer. Jesus Himself explained it: "I will not leave you as orphans; I will come to you…My Father will love him, and We will come to him and make Our abode with him" (John 14:18, 23).

From the beginning, God desired to dwell among His people; first in the garden, later in the tabernacle, and ultimately through His Son. Through Christ, that divine presence now resides not in buildings made with hands but in hearts made new.

Paul confirms this truth: "Do you not know that you are God's temple and that God's Spirit dwells in you?" (1 Corinthians 3:16). To be filled with the Spirit is to be filled with the living presence of God; His mind, His influence, His power.

The Spirit of truth guides, convicts, and empowers. It is the very breath of God animating His people. "Not by might, nor by power, but by My Spirit," says the Lord of hosts (Zechariah 4:6).

Doctrine – Understanding the Spirit's Work

The Holy Spirit is the shared life and influence of the Father and Son: the presence of God extended to humanity. It is divine mind and power in operation.

When Scripture speaks of being "filled with the Spirit," it means being

CHAPTER

EIGHT

THE SPIRIT OF TRUTH AND THE PRESENCE OF GOD

filled with God's presence until our own will is surrendered to His. The Spirit teaches, comforts, and strengthens because it is the personal ministry of Christ in the soul.

Ellen G. White described it beautifully: "Christ gives them the breath of His own Spirit, the life of His own life."[21]

True evangelism flows from purity before power. Before the Spirit empowered the disciples at Pentecost, the church was purified through repentance and unity. The Spirit cannot fill what sin controls. Scripture says, "Do not grieve the Holy Spirit of God" (Ephesians 4:30). Holiness prepares the vessel for power. A clean heart becomes the strongest channel for divine influence. The Spirit of truth never contradicts Scripture; it confirms it. Its mission is to glorify Christ (John 16:14), to lead us into all truth (John 16:13), and to produce fruit: "love, joy, peace, patience, kindness, goodness, faithfulness, gentleness, and self-control" (Galatians 5:22–23).

As Martyn Lloyd-Jones warned, the Spirit never leads believers apart from the Word He inspired.[22] The moment emotion or culture defines truth, the witness weakens. Phil Johnson described this harmony as the heart of evangelical conviction: Scripture as our foundation and the gospel as our center.[23][24] The Spirit of truth magnifies the Word of truth, never replacing it.[25]

When believers live under this influence, they reveal the very character of the Father. Obedience becomes natural because God Himself is at work within: "For it is God who works in you both to will and to do for His

21   Ellen G. White, *The Desire of Ages* (Mountain View, CA: Pacific Press, 1898), 827.

22 Lloyd-Jones, *The Christian Soldier*, 112.

23 Phil Johnson, 'Theology Matters,' *GraceLife Pulpit*, 2007.

24 Phil Johnson, "The Boundaries of Evangelicalism," *Grace to You Conference Series*, 2004, Session 2, transcript accessed 2025.

25 D. Martyn Lloyd-Jones, *What Is an Evangelical?* (Edinburgh: Banner of Truth Trust, 1992), 54–55.

good pleasure" (Philippians 2:13).

The early church understood that spiritual power was not emotional energy but divine enablement. Acts 4:31 records, "They were all filled with the Holy Spirit and continued to speak the word of God with boldness." The same Spirit who gave them courage empowers believers today, not for comfort, but for witness.

This is the mystery of godliness: not that we act holy in our own strength, but that God's holiness becomes active in us.

Practical Living – Walking in God's Presence

Walking in the Spirit is not an emotional high; it is a steady awareness of God's presence. It is living in harmony with divine purpose, whether on the job, at home, or in battle.

When the Spirit fills your life, you begin to think with Heaven's perspective. Anger gives way to patience, fear to faith, self to service. You no longer live merely reacting to the world; you act from divine impulse.

For the believer in uniform, this is where true strength lies. The Spirit steadies your hand when chaos rises, softens your tone when others are harsh, and reminds you that every act of mercy reflects your King.

To walk in the Spirit means to listen for the quiet conviction of God. Sometimes He restrains you from speaking; sometimes He urges you to move. Either way, His peace confirms His presence.

Cultivating this awareness requires time with God: in prayer, in His Word, and in quiet reflection. The more you commune with Him, the more naturally His thoughts become your own.

You may be the only reflection of Christ some people will ever see. When

His Spirit rules your life, your presence becomes an extension of His. That is evangelism in its purest form: God dwelling in human hearts and reaching others through them.

The measure of a Spirit-filled life is not noise or display, but endurance. Those who walk in God's presence keep shining when the crowd disperses. True spiritual strength is steady, humble obedience when no one sees but God.

Reflection – God With Us, God In Us

The greatest promise of Scripture is not simply forgiveness but fellowship; that God would dwell with His people. "Behold, the tabernacle of God is with men" (Revelation 21:3).

Each morning, renew that fellowship. Pray: "Father, live in me today through Your Spirit. Let Your presence govern my mind and Your peace fill my heart."

The Spirit of truth is not distant; it is as near as your next breath. It guides, comforts, corrects, and empowers. You are never alone because the life of God Himself flows within you. Let that presence define your thoughts, your words, and your actions. Then, wherever you go, others will sense the reality of Emmanuel; God with us.

When the Spirit of truth rules your life, you become a living witness that Heaven is near.

The Spirit's presence is not given for personal comfort alone but for divine commission. As Jesus said, "You will receive power when the Holy Spirit has come upon you, and you will be my witnesses" (Acts 1:8). The same presence that fills you sends you. His indwelling becomes your mission.

NINE

COMPASSION AND SERVICE: THE HEART OF EVANGELISM

Biblical Foundation

When Jesus walked among the people, His ministry was marked by compassion. "He was moved with compassion for them, because they were weary and scattered, like sheep having no shepherd" (Matthew 9:36). His healing touch, gentle words, and selfless service revealed the Father's love in a way no sermon alone could.

Throughout Scripture, God equates compassion with righteousness. Micah 6:8 declares, "What does the Lord require of you but to do justly, to love mercy, and to walk humbly with your God?" Compassion is not merely an emotion but an action; love expressed in deed.

In the parable of the Good Samaritan (Luke 10:30–37), Jesus defined true neighborly love. The priest and Levite passed by, absorbed in religious duty, but the Samaritan stopped, bound the wounds of the injured man, and provided for his recovery. Jesus concluded, "Go and do likewise."

This command is the heartbeat of evangelism: service done in the name of love. The gospel is never more convincing than when it is lived through kindness.

Doctrine – The Ministry of Compassion

Compassion is the visible evidence of divine presence. It is the Spirit of truth moving the believer to act as Christ would act. Jesus did not come merely to teach truth but to *embody* it; healing the sick, feeding the hungry, comforting the broken, and forgiving the lost.

Ellen White wrote, "Christ's method alone will give true success in reaching the people. The Savior mingled with men as one who desired their good. He showed His sympathy for them, ministered to their needs, and won their confidence."[26]

26   Ellen G. White, *The Ministry of Healing* (Mountain View, CA: Pacific Press, 1942), 143.

That same method is the model for every believer. True evangelism is not limited to preaching or public witnessing; it is the consistent expression of God's love through service.

The early Christians understood this principle. In Acts 2:44–47, they shared their possessions, cared for one another, and found favor with the people. Their compassion gave credibility to their message, and "the Lord added to the church daily those who were being saved."

Compassion validates truth. A heart transformed by God cannot remain indifferent to suffering. Where compassion is absent, witness loses its power.

When believers serve others out of genuine love, they reflect the heart of the Father. That reflection becomes the strongest form of evangelism: a living demonstration that the gospel changes not only what we believe but how we live.

Practical Living – Serving as Christ Served

To serve others is to represent Heaven in action. Compassion in daily life does not always mean large acts; often, it means small ones done with sincerity.

In health care, compassion listens when others rush. In law enforcement, compassion tempers judgment with understanding. In the military, compassion strengthens unity and morale. In every profession, compassion reminds the world that love is stronger than fear.

Look for the needs nearest to you: the elderly neighbor who lives alone, the coworker battling unseen stress, the struggling family in need of encouragement. Each act of kindness plants a seed of hope.

Service also guards the heart against selfishness. It shifts the focus from self to others, from convenience to calling. When you serve, you participate in the divine work of redemption.

You may never see the full result of your compassion, but God does. Every visit, every meal, every word of encouragement echoes through eternity. Jesus said, "Whatever you did for one of the least of these brothers and sisters of Mine, you did for Me" (Matthew 25:40).

Make compassion your habit. Let it flow naturally from a life filled with God's Spirit. The more you love others, the more Heaven becomes visible through you.

Reflection – Love in Action

The greatest sermon ever preached was not delivered from a pulpit but from a cross. There, divine compassion triumphed over sin and hate.

Every time we act in love, we honor that sacrifice. The world will not be reached by words alone but by hearts that mirror Christ's mercy.

Pray: "Father, make my hands instruments of Your compassion. Teach me to serve with humility, to listen with patience, and to love without measure."

True evangelism begins when our hearts beat with His; when the pain of others becomes our mission, and love becomes our message.

Compassion is not an option for the believer; it is the evidence of divine life within. It is Heaven's language spoken through human kindness.

Let your service preach louder than your speech. In doing so, you will reveal the heart of God to a world desperate to feel His touch.

CHAPTER
TEN

OBEDIENCE AND HOLINESS: THE WITNESS OF A TRANSFORMED LIFE

Biblical Foundation

The gospel that saves also sanctifies. Salvation is not the end of our calling but the beginning of transformation; a life that mirrors the holiness of God. Scripture says, "As He who called you is holy, you also be holy in all your conduct" (1 Peter 1:15).

Jesus declared, "If you love Me, keep My commandments" (John 14:15). Obedience is not the price of salvation but the proof of it. It is love made visible; the outward expression of an inward change.

The Bible consistently links obedience with faith. Abraham believed in God, and it was counted to him as righteousness; yet his faith was proven when he obeyed (Genesis 22:18). Likewise, the redeemed in Revelation are described as "those who keep the commandments of God and the faith of Jesus" (Revelation 14:12).

The world measures belief by words; Heaven measures it by fruit. "By their fruits, you will know them" (Matthew 7:20). True holiness is not perfection achieved by effort but submission perfected through grace; the life of Christ reproduced in the believer.

Doctrine – The Harmony of Grace and Obedience

Many misunderstand obedience as legalism, but Scripture reveals it as partnership. Grace provides the power; faith produces the action. "It is God who works in you both to will and to do for His good pleasure" (Philippians 2:13).

Holiness begins where self ends. It is the natural result of surrender, with the Spirit shaping our desires to reflect God's will. The law of God is no longer a set of restrictions but a revelation of His character, written not on stone but on the heart (Hebrews 8:10).

Ellen White wrote, "Obedience; the service and allegiance of love is the true sign of discipleship."[27] The believer who walks in obedience does so not to earn favor, but because grace has transformed the heart.

Holiness is not separation from the world in distance but in character. We live among others, yet not by their standards. The world's values no longer shape our decisions because our hearts are aligned with Heaven.

Obedience becomes a testimony. Every act of honesty, purity, forgiveness, and faithfulness declares, "God reigns in this life." In a world of compromise, holiness stands as quiet rebellion against sin.

Practical Living – The Daily Walk of Obedience

Obedience in daily life is revealed through consistency. It is how you respond when no one is watching, how you speak when wronged, and how you live when faced with temptation.

In the workplace, holiness means integrity, doing what is right even when shortcuts seem easier. In the home, it means patience and humility. In leadership, it means service instead of self-promotion.

Every believer faces tests of loyalty. The small choices, what we watch, how we speak, how we treat others, either draw us nearer to God or distance us from Him. The Spirit of truth convicts but never forces. Obedience is always voluntary, motivated by love.

As soldiers in God's service, we must maintain the discipline of the soul. Just as physical training strengthens the body, spiritual discipline strengthens faith. Prayer, study, and self-control are the believer's exercises of holiness.

---

27 Ellen G. White, *Steps to Christ* (Mountain View, CA: Pacific Press, 1892), 60.

Obedience also brings peace. When the heart is aligned with God's will, confusion fades. The conscience rests, knowing it walks in light. "Great peace have those who love Your law, and nothing causes them to stumble" (Psalm 119:165).

Reflection – The Beauty of a Holy Life

Holiness is not a burden; it is freedom, the freedom of living without duplicity, guilt, or compromise. It is walking in the light as He is in the light (1 John 1:7).

Pray daily: "Father, write Your law on my heart. Teach me to delight in Your will. Let my obedience reflect Your love."

A transformed life is the most convincing sermon the world will ever hear. You may never preach, but your conduct will testify.

True holiness is not achieved through effort but received through surrender. The Spirit of God makes obedience joyful and holiness possible.

When others see calm where there should be anger, faith where there should be fear, and purity where there should be pride, they witness the miracle of a transformed heart.

Holiness is Heaven's signature on the soul. It tells the world: *God lives here.*

Holiness prepares the heart for communion. To sustain the life of obedience, we must learn to walk continually in God's presence through prayer.

CHAPTER

ELEVEN

THE POWER OF PRAYER AND PRESENCE: STAYING CLOSE TO THE SOURCE

Biblical Foundation

Before Jesus preached to the crowds or healed the sick, He prayed. Luke records that "He withdrew to desolate places and prayed" (Luke 5:16). Prayer was not an interruption to His ministry; it was the foundation of it.

When the disciples asked, *"Lord, teach us to pray,"* (Luke 11:1), they weren't looking for ritual words. They had seen the power that flowed from His communion with the Father.

Prayer connects mission to power.

Before Pentecost, before miracles, before missions, the early church prayed. Acts 1:14 says, *"All these with one accord were devoting themselves to prayer."* Then came the outpouring of the Spirit and the birth of the church's witness. Prayer doesn't prepare us for ministry, prayer is ministry.

Doctrine: Prayer as the Breath of Evangelism

Evangelism without prayer is like breathing without air; it cannot live.

Prayer is the unseen force that gives life to every act of witness. Through prayer, we receive courage, discernment, and compassion.

Jesus said, *"Apart from Me you can do nothing."* (John 15:5).

Prayer is our confession of that truth. It keeps us dependent on God rather than on talent or strategy.

The Holy Spirit is the true evangelist. He convicts hearts, opens doors, and guides conversations that we could never plan. Our part is to stay close enough to God that His Spirit can speak through us when the moment comes.

Sometimes prayer itself **is** evangelism. When words fail or doors close, intercession becomes the mission field. To pray for someone is to fight for their soul in unseen places. Heaven moves when believers kneel.

Practical Living: Ministry Through Prayer and Presence

In a noisy world, presence is powerful. You don't always need eloquence; you need empathy.

- Pray Before You Go:

Before each shift, meeting, or task, ask God to go before you.

You may never know how He arranges circumstances, but prayer ensures you carry His peace instead of your pressure.

- Pray for Those You Meet:

Every person you encounter carries unseen burdens. Whisper simple prayers like, *"Lord, bless them. Heal them. Reveal Yourself to them."*

These small petitions invite heaven into ordinary moments.

- Be Present:

Sometimes evangelism is not about saying the right thing but simply being there.

Jesus' presence brought calm to storms and comfort to sorrow.

Your patience, listening ear, or quiet strength can speak Christ more powerfully than many words.

- Intercede for the Lost:

Don't underestimate what happens when you consistently pray for others.

Those who resist your words cannot outrun your prayers.

Prayer is not wasted effort, it is the groundwork of grace.

Reflection: Staying Close to the Source

The power of an evangelist lies not in effort, but in intimacy with God.

Before you go out, go up. Before you speak to people, speak to Him.

The more time you spend in His presence, the more naturally His presence will flow through you.

When you pray, heaven listens. When you are present, God is visible.

When both combine, prayer and presence, lives change quietly but eternally.

Let your prayer life be your preparation, and your presence be your preaching.

Stay near the Source, and the Spirit will sustain you.

CHAPTER

TWELVE

TRIALS, REFINEMENT, AND THE DISCIPLINE OF GOD'S LOVE

Biblical Foundation

The Christian life is not free from hardship; it is refined by it. Scripture declares, "Whom the Lord loves, He disciplines, and scourges every son whom He receives" (Hebrews 12:6). The trials we face are not signs of abandonment but of belonging.

Throughout the Bible, God's people were refined through affliction. Joseph was shaped by years of injustice before becoming a deliverer. David fled through caves before sitting on a throne. Daniel faced lions before ruling with wisdom. Every test became a testimony.

Peter wrote, "Beloved, do not think it strange concerning the fiery trial which is to try you, as though some strange thing happened to you; but rejoice, inasmuch as you are partakers of Christ's sufferings" (1 Peter 4:12–13). Trials are not accidents; they are divine appointments designed to reveal what remains unrefined within us.

Gold is purified by fire, and so are souls. God allows circumstances that strip away self-dependence, pride, and fear until only faith remains. "He will sit as a refiner and purifier of silver" (Malachi 3:3).

The purpose of discipline is not punishment but restoration. Through hardship, God corrects our course, deepens our trust, and brings forth character that reflects His own.

Doctrine – God's Refining Process

Discipline is the education of Heaven. It is how God trains His children for eternity. Just as a soldier endures training to prepare for battle, believers endure trials to develop endurance, humility, and faith.

God's correction is an expression of His love, not His anger. "For whom the Lord loves, He corrects, just as a father the son in whom he delights" (Proverbs 3:12). A loving father disciplines not to destroy but to strengthen.

The refining process removes impurities that cannot enter Heaven. Ellen White wrote, "The trials of life are God's workmen to remove the impurities and roughness from our character." (Steps to Christ, p. 57). The Spirit works through hardship to reveal areas where surrender is incomplete.

Discipline is not always dramatic. Sometimes it comes in the form of delay, disappointment, or correction through His Word. Every challenge invites us to yield more deeply to His will.

True refinement brings balance. We learn to trust when we cannot see, to endure when we cannot understand, and to praise even in pain. That is the maturity of faith, obedience without explanation.

Practical Living – Growing Through Hardship

Trials often come where we least expect them, in relationships, finances, leadership, or personal struggle. But each one has a purpose. They are tools God uses to strengthen spiritual muscle and prove the reality of our faith.

In law enforcement or military service, discipline is essential. It builds endurance and readiness. Likewise, spiritual discipline trains the believer to stand firm under pressure. Prayer becomes the daily drill that fortifies the mind. Scripture becomes the armor that shields the heart.

When difficulty comes, resist the urge to ask, *"Why me?"* Instead, ask, *"What are You teaching me?"*

Each hardship carries a hidden lesson. Failure teaches humility, loss deepens compassion, and endurance produces strength. What the enemy means for harm, God transforms for growth.

Practical faith is forged in the fire of adversity. As you face challenges, remember that God's goal is not your comfort but your completeness. The trial is temporary, but the character it builds is eternal.

Reflection – Purified for Purpose

When you walk through the fire, remember who controls the flame. The same God who allows the trial sets its limit. He knows how long and how hot it must be to refine your faith without consuming your hope.

Pray: "Father, help me trust Your process. Teach me to see Your hand even in hardship, and let every trial draw me nearer to You."

Discipline is not rejection; it is restoration. It is God's way of saying, *"You are mine, and I will not leave you as you are."*

Every test you pass strengthens the witness of your life. Others may see only your endurance, but Heaven sees gold emerging from the fire.

When you endure with faith, you preach without words. Your perseverance declares that God is worthy of trust even when life hurts.

The believer refined by trial becomes a vessel fit for divine purpose: strong, pure, and filled with His presence.

Let your scars tell the story of grace, not defeat. For every mark of testing is also a mark of love.

Refinement shapes individuals, but revival multiplies through community. God's mission is never carried by one voice alone; it thrives when His people unite in witness.

CHAPTER
THIRTEEN

BUILDING A COMMUNITY OF WITNESSES: THE STRENGTH OF SHARED MISSION

Biblical Foundation

When Jesus sent out His disciples, He sent them *two by two* (Mark 6:7).

That small detail reveals a timeless truth: the Gospel was never meant to be carried alone.

From the very beginning, God declared, *"It is not good that man should be alone."* (Genesis 2:18).

Humanity was created for fellowship, and the Church was built for team-work.

Acts 2:44–47 paints a picture of the early believers: "All who believed were together and had all things in common… They broke bread in their homes and ate together with glad and sincere hearts."

Their unity became their testimony. It drew others in, not by marketing or programs, but by the visible power of love in community.

Evangelism flourishes through relationships. One believer may light a spark, but together, the Church becomes a beacon.

Doctrine: The Fellowship of the Commissioned

The Church is not an audience; it is an army.

Paul described believers as *"one body with many members, each having different gifts."* (1 Corinthians 12:12–27)

Unity does not erase individuality; it redeems it for a shared purpose.

Hebrews 10:24–25 reminds us:

"Let us consider how to stir up one another to love and good works, not neglecting to meet together."

Community evangelism strengthens both the message and the messenger.

It offers encouragement, accountability, and protection from discouragement.

When hearts are united under one mission, to make Christ known, the Spirit moves in power.

Isolation weakens the believer, but fellowship fortifies the mission.

The enemy scatters; God gathers.

Each time believers pray, serve, and celebrate together, they proclaim the unity of heaven in a divided world.

Practical Living: Working Together in the Mission Field

Evangelism is not competition; it is cooperation. The harvest is plentiful, but it takes a team to gather it (Matthew 9:37–38).

Here's what teamwork in evangelism looks like:

- In the Church:

Encourage and equip one another. Start prayer groups, mentoring circles, or outreach teams.

Every gathering can become a launching point for mission.

- In the Workplace:

When two or three believers unite in faith, the environment changes.

Shared integrity, prayer, and kindness can quietly shift the culture around them.

- In the Community:

Service projects, feeding the hungry, visiting the sick, mentoring youth are living sermons.

When believers collaborate in compassion, the world sees Christ in action.

- In Family Life:

A household united in faith becomes a small church.

When spouses, children, and relatives serve together, faith grows stronger across generations.

The strength of a Christian community lies not in perfection but in purpose.

Even small groups can change cities when love drives their mission.

Reflection: Strength in Togetherness

The Gospel is not a solo journey. You are part of a body; a family of believers chosen to carry light together.

If you ever feel alone in your faith, remember Elijah.

He thought he was the only prophet left, but God reminded him that *seven thousand others had not bowed to Baal* (1 Kings 19:18).

God always has more witnesses than you can see.

Community keeps faith alive when personal strength fades.

Fellowship multiplies courage when fear whispers that your efforts don't matter.

The Church is not a crowd of spectators; it is a company of ambassadors.

Link arms with fellow believers. Pray with them. Serve beside them.

Encourage one another to keep going when the world grows dark.

When believers unite in mission, heaven smiles, for unity among God's people is one of His greatest testimonies to the world.

Together, we are stronger.

Together, we are brighter.

Together, we are commissioned.

Community gives strength to the message; urgency gives speed to the mission.

CHAPTER
FOURTEEN

THE URGENCY OF THE MESSAGE: PREPARING FOR THE FINAL HARVEST

Biblical Foundation

From Genesis to Revelation, Scripture portrays the work of God as a great harvest. Time moves toward a divine conclusion when the seeds of faith and rebellion alike will yield their final fruit. Jesus said, "The harvest is the end of the world, and the reapers are the angels" (Matthew 13:39).

The prophets spoke of this moment with solemn clarity. Joel declared, "Put in the sickle, for the harvest is ripe…Multitudes, multitudes in the valley of decision! For the day of the Lord is near" (Joel 3:13–14).

In Revelation, John sees an angel "having the everlasting gospel to preach to those who dwell on the earth…saying with a loud voice, 'Fear God and give glory to Him, for the hour of His judgment has come'" (Revelation 14:6–7). This is not a message of fear, but of awakening: a call to return to obedience, reverence, and readiness.

The urgency of evangelism rests in this truth: time is short, but grace still pleads. Every act of kindness, every word of truth, every life lived for Christ adds to the great gathering of souls before the close of probation.

We are not only witnesses of Christ's love but heralds of His soon return. The gospel of the kingdom "will be preached in all the world as a witness to all nations, and then the end will come" (Matthew 24:14).

Doctrine – The Final Message of Hope and Warning

The everlasting gospel carries both mercy and warning. It calls humanity to worship the Creator, to reject the deceptions of Babylon, and to remain faithful to God's commandments. This is the threefold message of Revelation 14: a declaration to the whole earth before the harvest.

Ellen White described this message as "the most solemn warning ever given to mortals" and yet "the most hopeful, for it reveals Christ's power to save" (Testimonies, Vol. 6, p. 19).

The first angel's message summons us to reverence and worship the true God, the Creator of heaven and earth. The second warns against false systems of worship and self-exaltation. The third calls for endurance: "Here is the patience of the saints: here are they that keep the commandments of God and the faith of Jesus" (Revelation 14:12).

This prophetic framework is not a symbolic theory, but a moral reality. It reminds us that every generation faces the same test: loyalty to God or conformity to the world. The "mark on the forehead or hand" (Revelation 14:9) represents a choice, either submission to divine truth or surrender to human authority.

The final harvest depends on the faithfulness of laborers today. God entrusts His message not to angels alone but to human messengers, to believers in every nation and profession who live and proclaim His truth with conviction.

Practical Living – Working While It Is Day

Jesus said, "We must work the works of Him who sent Me while it is day; night is coming, when no one can work" (John 9:4). The urgency of the gospel does not call for panic but for purpose. Every believer must live with eternal awareness, using every opportunity to sow seeds of truth.

For the soldier, it may be courage under fire. For the officer, justice tempered with mercy. For the nurse, compassion toward the forgotten. For the teacher, truth spoken in love. Every intentional act becomes part of the harvest.

The final message will not be carried by famous preachers alone but by faithful believers who live the gospel where they stand. The power of the

Spirit will rest upon those whose hearts are surrendered, whose voices speak truth with humility, and whose lives reveal God's law of love.

To live in these final days is to live on mission. The call of the hour is clear: to awaken from complacency, to renew our commitment to obedience, and to labor for souls while grace still invites. The fields are white. Heaven waits for willing hands.

Reflection – Living for the Last Call

We stand on the edge of eternity. The events of prophecy unfold swiftly, and every day brings us closer to the great harvest. Yet even now, mercy lingers. The Spirit of God still pleads with hearts, still calls sinners home, still empowers the church to labor in love.

Ask yourself: *If Christ were to return today, would I be found faithful in my field?* Do not wait for a perfect moment to serve; every day is a divine appointment. Share truth while there is time. Live the gospel openly, love others deeply, and let your life proclaim the message: *"The Lord is coming; prepare to meet Him."*

Pray: "Father, give me urgency without fear, courage without pride, and compassion without delay. Let me labor faithfully until the final harvest is gathered." The day will come when the sowing will cease and the reaping will begin. Until then, live as one who knows the season: awake, alert, and anointed for the final call. Your time is now. The harvest is near. What we begin with urgency, we must finish with endurance.

CHAPTER
FIFTEEN

FINISHING THE RACE FAITHFULLY: PERSEVERANCE IN THE CALL

Biblical Foundation

Near the end of his life, the Apostle Paul wrote,

"I have fought the good fight, I have finished the race, I have kept the faith." (2 Timothy 4:7)

These are not words of regret, but of triumph, the voice of a man who remained faithful through every trial.

Shipwrecks, prison, hunger, rejection, none of it silenced his testimony because his eyes were fixed on eternity.

Paul understood that faithfulness, not fame, is the true measure of a life devoted to Christ.

The believer's journey is not a sprint; it is a marathon of grace.

It requires focus, endurance, and trust in the One who called us.

The Great Commission was never meant to be a temporary assignment, it lasts until the last breath of the faithful servant.

Doctrine: Endurance as the Mark of the Called

Scripture is clear: *"The one who endures to the end will be saved."* (Matthew 24:13).

The Christian life is defined not by how passionately it begins, but by how steadfastly it continues.

Faithful evangelism is not about visible results; it's about persistent obedience.

There will be seasons of fruitfulness and seasons of silence, moments of victory and times of waiting.

Yet God calls us to remain steadfast through them all.

The Bible compares faith to a race not run for human applause, but for an eternal crown (1 Corinthians 9:25).

That crown is not reserved for pastors or missionaries alone; it belongs to every believer who finishes their calling with integrity and humility.

The same Spirit who began the work in you will sustain it until the end (Philippians 1:6).

Faithfulness may not be glamorous, but it is glorious in heaven's eyes.

Practical Living: Running with Purpose

Every believer has a race to run, uniquely marked out by God.

Yours may lead through classrooms, hospitals, patrol cars, or homes, but the finish line is the same: to hear, *"Well done, good and faithful servant."* (Matthew 25:21)

Here's how to run well:

- Keep Your Eyes on Christ:

When we fixate on outcomes or recognition, discouragement sets in.

Focus on the One who called you, not the size of the crowd that follows you.

- Pace Yourself with Prayer:

Prayer keeps the spirit steady and renews strength when fatigue sets in. You cannot run long distances without constant communion with the Source.

- Encourage Others Along the Way:

The race was never meant to be lonely. Helping others finish strengthens your own endurance.

- Lay Aside Distractions:

Hebrews 12:1 reminds us to "throw off everything that hinders."

Let go of resentment, pride, or comparison; they slow the steps of faith.

- Rest When Needed, but Never Quit:

Even Jesus rested. True endurance is not constant motion but constant devotion.

To finish the race faithfully means to love when it's hard, to serve when unseen, and to keep believing when nothing seems to change.

Your perseverance might be someone else's proof that God is real.

Reflection: The Reward of Faithfulness

At the end of the journey, God will not ask how many people praised you, but how many times you said "yes" to His call.

Every act of kindness, every moment of courage, every prayer whispered in faith has eternal weight.

When you stumble, rise again.

When you grow weary, rest in Him.

When you feel unseen, remember heaven is watching.

The race is not over until the trumpet sounds at the ressurection and the Lord calls you home (1 Corinthians 15:52; 1 Thessalonians 4:16). Until then, keep running with joy, keep serving with love, and keep standing with courage.

You are commissioned not only to begin the work, but to finish it faith-fully.

Run until you see His face.

That is the victory of the believer.

CHAPTER

SIXTEEN

LIVING COMMISSIONED: THE CALL TO CONTINUE THE WORK

Biblical Foundation

Before His ascension, Jesus gave His disciples their lifelong purpose: "Go therefore and make disciples of all nations…teaching them to observe all that I have commanded you; and lo, I am with you always, even to the end of the world" (Matthew 28:19–20).

This was not a suggestion; it was a commissioning. It did not end with the apostles; it continues through every believer who carries the name of Christ.

The same Spirit that empowered the early church empowers us today. The promise of Acts 1:8 remains: "You shall receive power when the Holy Spirit has come upon you, and you shall be My witnesses…to the end of the earth."

To live commissioned is to live in obedience to this command. It is to see the world through the eyes of Christ and not as a collection of strangers, but as a field ready for harvest. Every believer is a missionary, every home a mission post, and every profession a pulpit.

The Great Commission is not complete until every believer recognizes their personal role in it.

Doctrine – The Continuation of Christ's Mission

Christ came not only to redeem humanity but to reproduce His ministry through His followers. "As the Father has sent Me, even so I send you" (John 20:21). The mission of the church is the extension of the ministry of Christ.

The early disciples understood this. They went out preaching, teaching, healing, and serving. They were not professionals but participants: fishermen, tax collectors, tentmakers, all filled with divine purpose. Their power was not in status but in surrender.

Ellen White wrote, "Every true disciple is born into the kingdom of God as a missionary" (Desire of Ages, p. 195). This means evangelism is not an option for a few, but the calling of all.

To live commissioned is to live aware that every conversation, every act of kindness, and every moment of faithfulness is a continuation of Christ's work.

The same Spirit that moved through Him now moves through His people. The gospel advances not through programs, but through presence: believers filled with God's Spirit, living the message of reconciliation wherever they go.

Practical Living – Your Life as a Mission

Living commissioned does not require a pulpit or passport. It begins with a willing heart.

Ask yourself: *Where has God already placed me to serve?* Your job, your family, your community; these are your mission fields.

In the military, the phrase "stand to your post" means to remain faithful to your duty until relieved. The same is true spiritually. God assigns each believer a field of influence. Our task is to stand faithfully, work diligently, and shine continually.

Each morning, dedicate your day to service. Say, "Father, this day is Yours. Let every word and action represent You." This simple act transforms ordinary routines into sacred opportunities.

To live commissioned means to love without condition, serve without reward, and witness without fear. It means standing firm in truth, even when others fall away.

Some are called to preach publicly; others are called to witness quietly. Both are essential. The gospel moves through the hands of those who serve, the mouths of those who speak, and the hearts of those who pray.

Remember: you may be the only reflection of Christ someone will ever see. Live so that His character is unmistakable in you.

Reflection – Until the Work Is Finished

The mission of Christ did not end at Calvary; it continues through His people today. Heaven still waits for a generation who will live fully surrendered, fully committed, and fully commissioned. Pray: "Lord, here am I; send me. Use my life, my words, and my work to reveal You to others."

To live commissioned is to wake each day with purpose. It is to know that eternity touches every moment of obedience. It is to live not for applause but for impact.

You have not been called to comfort but to God's purposeful assignment for you; not to spectatorship but to service. The same power that raised Jesus from the dead lives in you.

So stand to your post. Speak the truth in love. Serve with compassion. Shine in the darkness. The world will know Christ through lives that are wholly His.

The Great Commission is still in motion, and you are part of it.

Live commissioned, today, tomorrow, and until the work is done.

EPILOGUE – A LIFE COMMISSIONED

You were not born by accident. You were created with purpose, redeemed with intention, and sent with a mission. The same God who called prophets and apostles now calls you, not necessarily to foreign lands, but to faithfulness where you stand.

The Great Commission was never meant to rest on a few shoulders. It was given to the body of Christ: every believer, every worker, every servant. Wherever there is life, there is ministry.

When you understand this truth, evangelism stops being a program and becomes a lifestyle. It becomes the way you walk, speak, and love. It becomes the quiet prayer before your shift, the patience in your tone, the compassion in your eyes.

To be commissioned is to live aware that Heaven is watching, that the Spirit is guiding, and that eternity is moving through your daily steps. The Christian life is not a waiting room for Heaven; it is the training ground for service.

When Christ ascended, He did not retire His work; He multiplied it. Through His Spirit, He continues His ministry in the world through us. Every believer is an extension of His compassion, His truth, and His power.

Your badge, your uniform, your hands: all belong to Him. Your influence, your story, and your testimony are all tools in the hands of the Master.

There is no greater calling than this: to be a vessel through which the living God touches lives. The fields are still white. The laborers are still few. The world is still searching for light.

But God still sends.

So take your post with courage. Stand in your calling with humility. Speak truth with love. Serve with joy. And when your work is finished, you will hear the words that every faithful laborer longs for: "Well done, good and faithful servant…enter into the joy of your Lord" (Matthew 25:23).

You are not waiting to be sent.

You already are.

Live commissioned until the whole world knows the love of Christ.`

ABOUT THE AUTHOR

Michael A. Reahl lives and serves in Alaska, where faith and service intersect in everyday life. A U.S. Army National Guard Infantry Officer and Police Officer, Michael has built his ministry on the front lines of both public safety and spiritual leadership. His calling is simple yet profound: to live the gospel where life happens and to help others see that every field of duty is a mission field.

He holds a Master of Theological Studies and a Bachelor of Science in Public Health, combining biblical knowledge with real-world experience in leadership, wellness, and community care. He has also served as a lifeguard trainer, medical instructor, and educator in prehospital emergency medicine, teaching courses such as CPR, ACLS, PALS, NRP, ITLS, and PHTLS.

Michael's background in both the military and medical fields has shaped his deep conviction that evangelism is not confined to pulpits or sanctuaries. Whether leading a team, training first responders, or standing watch in uniform, he sees every act of service as a reflection of God's presence.

Beyond his professional and ministry roles, Michael has participated in mission work around the world, including in Ghana, Mexico, Cambodia, Mongolia, and other nations. There, he has witnessed the power of the gospel to heal, unify, and transform. He also served as a colporteur, sharing Christian literature door to door, learning firsthand that the most meaningful ministry often begins with a simple conversation.

Through his writing and teaching, Michael seeks to awaken believers to their personal calling to evangelism. His passion is to remind readers that ministry belongs to every Christian, regardless of title or training, that faith must be lived as well as spoken.

In *Commissioned: God's Call to Every Believer, Not Just the Pastor*, Michael invites readers to rediscover what it means to be sent, to live as ambassadors of the Kingdom in workplaces, communities, and every corner of daily life.

BIBLIOGRAPHY

The following works provided insight, inspiration, and theological foundation for this book. While this text stands as a personal reflection on practical evangelism, it draws strength from timeless writings that have shaped Christian thought and mission throughout history.

Primary Sources and References

The Holy Bible – English Standard Version (ESV).

Bauer, Walter. A Greek-English Lexicon of the New Testament and Other Early Christian Literature. University of Chicago Press, 1958.

Brunn, Dave. *One Bible, Many Versions: Are All Translations Created Equal?* InterVarsity Press, 2013.

Green, Michael. *Evangelism in the Early Church.* Wm. B. Eerdmans Publishing Co., 2004.

Johnson, Phil. *Theology Matters.* GraceLife, 2007.

Johnson, Phil. "The Boundaries of Evangelicalism." *Grace to You Conference Series,* 2004, Session 2 (transcript accessed 2025).

Kreider, Alan. *The Patient Ferment of the Early Church.* Baker Academic, 2016.

Lloyd-Jones, D. Martyn. *What Is an Evangelical?* Edinburgh: Banner of Truth Trust, 1992.

Lloyd-Jones, Martyn. *The Christian Soldier: Standing Firm in the Faith.* Grand Rapids, MI: Baker Books, 2003.

Lloyd-Jones, Martyn. *Preaching & Preachers.* Grand Rapids, MI:

Zondervan, 1971.

Lloyd-Jones, Martyn. *Joy Unspeakable: Power & Renewal in the Holy Spirit.* Wheaton, IL: Crossway, 1984.

Paulsen, Jan. *When the Spirit Descends.* Pacific Press, 1998.

Reid, Alvin. *Introduction to Evangelism.* Nashville, TN: B&H Publishing Group, 1998.

Webber, Robert E. *The Younger Evangelicals: Facing the Challenges of the New World.* Baker Books, 2002.

White, Ellen G. *Evangelism.* Review and Herald Publishing Association, 2002.

White, Ellen G. *A Call to Medical Evangelism and Health Education.* TEACH Services, Inc., 1997.

White, Ellen G. *The Desire of Ages.* Mountain View, CA: Pacific Press, 1898.

White, Ellen G. *The Ministry of Healing.* Mountain View, CA: Pacific Press, 1905.

White, Ellen G. *Steps to Christ.* Washington, D.C.: Review and Herald, 1892.

Supplementary and Historical Sources

Ellen G. White. *Steps to Christ.* Review and Herald, 1892.

Ellen G. White. *The Desire of Ages.* Pacific Press, 1898.

Ellen G. White. *Ministry of Healing.* Pacific Press, 1905.

Ellen G. White. *Testimonies for the Church*, Vol. 6. Review and Herald,

1901.

J.N. Andrews. *History of the Sabbath and the First Day of the Week.* Steam Press, 1873.

James White. *Gospel Order.* Review and Herald, 1854.

Uriah Smith. *Daniel and the Revelation.* Review and Herald, 1897.

SCRIPTURE INDEX

This section lists all Scripture references cited throughout the book in order of appearance, arranged by biblical book.

Old Testament

Exodus – 3:5

Deuteronomy – 8:7–10

Psalms – 65:9–13

Proverbs – 4:18

Isaiah – 60:1–3

Zechariah – 4:6

New Testament

Matthew – 5:16; 8; 20:28; 25:35–36; 28:19–20

Mark – 16:15

Luke – 4:36; 8:39; 15:10; 17:10

John – 3:16; 4:35; 8:26; 10:35; 14:23; 20:21

Acts – 1:8; 2:41; 4:20; 4:29–31; 5:41–42; 8:4; 20:20

Romans – 8:9–11; 12:2; 13:11

1 Corinthians – 7:17; 15:3–4

2 Corinthians – 3:3; 5:17; 5:18; 5:20

Galatians – 6:9

Ephesians – 4:12; 6:14

Colossians – 3:23; 4:6

Philippians – 1:6; 2:13; 4:6–9

Hebrews – 1:14

1 Peter – 1:15; 2:12; 4:12–13

Revelation – 14:6–12